THE
LOVER'S
BOOK

Also by Genny Wright Davis
and Bruce Davis, Ph.D.

Hugs and Kisses
The Magical Child Within You

THE LOVER'S BOOK

YOUR SECRET SOURCE OF LOVE

Genny Wright Davis and Bruce Davis, Ph.D.

Illustrated by Genny Wright Davis

MACMILLAN PUBLISHING CO., INC. • New York

Macmillan Publishing Co., Inc.
866 Third Avenue, New York, N.Y. 10022
Collier Macmillan Canada, Ltd.

Library of Congress Cataloging in Publication Data
Davis, Genny Wright
The lover's book.
1. Love. 2. Self-acceptance. I. Davis, Bruce
joint author. II. Title.
BF575.L8D354   158'.2   79-21076
ISBN 0-02-529860-7

First Printing 1980

Printed in the United States of America

We would like to
dedicate this book to our
grandmothers, who have
shared with us
what love and friendship
are all about.

THE
LOVER'S
BOOK

There is lots and lots
of love in this world,
but sometimes
it's hard to feel it.

The more
you look around,
the more
you try to find it,
the more desperate
and lonely
you seem to become.

You see couples loving each other, but can't help feeling something is missing.

Some couples
love each other
but have trouble
being together.

Other couples
simply avoid one another.

There are the people
who don't like themselves
who choose someone who
does not like them either.

Some people
are hopelessly committed
to their partner.

Sometimes
one partner
is too busy—

Or the circumstances
are just never right—

Or you discover
he has some strange habit—

Or neither partner
can agree on sex—

So you break up

Or remain undecided and stay in between many relationships.

Some people
go from one relationship
to another
instead of looking at
what's going on inside

Or go to party
after party
looking for someone new

Or go it alone
and try to remain cool.

There are those
who embrace
a far-out philosophy,
convinced this will
provide the love
they have always sought.

Some people travel
to faraway islands
in search of
that special person.

And some people spend
all hours of the night
studying, forgetting
the love they really want.

While others look
for it at the end of
a fork or at
the bottom of a glass.

It seems you have tried everything and nothing works.

Do you settle
for nothing and feel
alone and empty?

No!
This is the time
to remember you're never
really alone.
A very special part of you
is always with you.

It's the part of you
that only feelings
can describe—
it's your heart.

What you are looking for
is already within you.
But you say,
"I want a relationship,
someone to love
and play with,
someone who understands.
How can I feel that
inside of me?"

Well, why not begin by
giving to yourself, by
noticing all the
special things
you already have?

Instead of trying
to love someone else,
why not start
by loving yourself?

Why not take the chain
off your leg
and become committed
to yourself instead?

Giving yourself
the attention
you always wanted
makes the lack of love
you feel from others
less important
because you and yourself
have become partners.

Give yourself nice walks,
flowers, toys, champagne,
or anything else
that makes you happy.

Or go into your room
and hug your favorite
stuffed animal,
letting the child within
you come out and play.

Loving yourself
may be sitting down
for a good cry,
letting your feelings
have their way.

These are the times
to remember that
special voice within you
and know it is always there
to love and to guide you.

Why not give yourself
some of the love
you always wanted?

You deserve it!

And once you really
love yourself, you have
so much more love
to give someone else.

You have been growing
and trusting
and now you are ready
for two to grow
and trust together.

In a family,
on a date,
or standing alone,
life is blooming
and you feel full.

You have found the love
in your heart
that makes you whole.

Now it's time
for your dreams,
because dreams
are not only for dreaming
but to come true.

It's time for your love
to be shared,
now that you believe
more and more in you.